Apress Pocket Guides

Apress Pocket Guides present concise summaries of cutting-edge developments and working practices throughout the tech industry. Shorter in length, books in this series aim to deliver quick-to-read guides that are easy to absorb, perfect for the time-poor professional.

This series covers the full spectrum of topics relevant to the modern industry, from security, AI, machine learning, cloud computing, web development, product design, to programming techniques and business topics too.

Typical topics might include:

- A concise guide to a particular topic, method, function or framework

- Professional best practices and industry trends

- A snapshot of a hot or emerging topic

- Industry case studies

- Concise presentations of core concepts suited for students and those interested in entering the tech industry

- Short reference guides outlining 'need-to-know' concepts and practices.

More information about this series at https://link.springer.com/bookseries/17385.

Building IoT Systems

Design Scalable IoT Systems from Edge to Cloud

Avirup Basu

Apress®

Building IoT Systems: Design Scalable IoT Systems from Edge to Cloud

Avirup Basu
Siliguri, West Bengal, India

ISBN-13 (pbk): 979-8-8688-1211-8   ISBN-13 (electronic): 979-8-8688-1212-5
https://doi.org/10.1007/979-8-8688-1212-5

Copyright © 2025 by Avirup Basu

Managing Director, Apress Media LLC: Welmoed Spahr
Acquisitions Editor: Spandana Chatterjee
Development Editor: James Markham
Editorial Assistant: Gryffin Winkler

Cover designed by eStudioCalamar

Distributed to the book trade worldwide by Springer Science+Business Media New York, 1 New York Plaza, New York, NY 10004. Phone 1-800-SPRINGER, fax (201) 348-4505, e-mail orders-ny@springer-sbm.com, or visit www.springeronline.com. Apress Media, LLC is a Delaware LLC and the sole member (owner) is Springer Science + Business Media Finance Inc (SSBM Finance Inc). SSBM Finance Inc is a **Delaware** corporation.

For information on translations, please e-mail booktranslations@springernature.com; for reprint, paperback, or audio rights, please e-mail bookpermissions@springernature.com.

Apress titles may be purchased in bulk for academic, corporate, or promotional use. eBook versions and licenses are also available for most titles. For more information, reference our Print and eBook Bulk Sales web page at http://www.apress.com/bulk-sales.

Any source code or other supplementary material referenced by the author in this book is available to readers on GitHub. For more detailed information, please visit https://www.apress.com/gp/services/source-code.

If disposing of this product, please recycle the paper

Table of Contents

About the Author

 **Avirup Basu** is a technologist, founder, and a digital transformation and innovation leader based out of India. He is the CEO & Founder of Blackspektro, which specialises in industrial IoT and AI solutions for manufacturing. The focus is on enabling digital transformation from the factory floor to the cloud.

He was previously working at P360 in various roles and stepped down after 8 years as an Associate Principal Engineer. He was responsible for designing and developing SaaS products like Swittons and Zing. These products transform enterprise workflows and real-time communication through smart devices and software platforms.

Drawing on over 9 years of experience in cloud systems, and event-driven architectures and industrial and commercial IoT, he builds scalable, resilient platforms that deliver real value in complex environments.

Outside of work, he organizes Google Developer Group (GDG) Siliguri, where he mentors and engages with the tech community through meetups and workshops.

When he isn't working on product or code, he spends time cycling, capturing moments through photography and videography, rallying for a game of tennis, or chasing adrenaline through adventure sports. He believes a sharp mind needs a spirited life.

About the Technical Reviewer

Atonu Ghosh is a Ph.D. research scholar in the Department of Computer Science and Engineering at the Indian Institute of Technology Kharagpur, West Bengal, India. He also has an M.Tech. and a B.Tech. in Computer Science and Engineering. Atonu's research domain includes the Internet of Things (IoT), edge computing, low power networks, and Industry 4.0. Atonu has built IoT solutions for over eight years and has executed several projects. He is also an active reviewer of research journals and books. Find out more about Atonu or reach him through his personal website https://www.atonughosh.com.

CHAPTER 1

Internet of Things: The Beginning of a Smarter World

Smart devices surround the world we live in. From devices we use almost regularly to highly complex systems, IoT (or the Internet of Things) is everywhere. When discussing IoT, the first thing that comes to mind is hardware, but if we look from a broader perspective, it's not just hardware. It combines many components, of which hardware is just one part. Essentially, IoT is not just hardware.

Then, the first question that comes to our mind is what exactly is IoT, or how do we define it?

To keep it simple, IoT is a system where devices communicate with each other or with other systems like cell phones, servers or more. The following terms are used throughout the book and will help put the discussions in context:

- Thing: Any physical device that can connect to any network and exchange information by sending or receiving data.

- Edge device: A physical device that can perform some form of processing. All edge devices are things, but not all things are edge devices.

© Avirup Basu 2025
A. Basu, *Building IoT Systems*, Apress Pocket Guides,
https://doi.org/10.1007/979-8-8688-1212-5_1

- Network: In the case of IoT, a network can be referred to as a local network or a vast area network, or sometimes we may refer to a simple RF network.

- Cloud computing: We can host applications and run services on these platforms. It's a key component and will be used throughout the book.

Let's start our journey on IoT by understanding the basics. These might seem simple, but they will be the foundation for more advanced concepts and implementations.

Reviewing the Basics

Like any network-based application, the world of IoT revolves around the general networking concept. IoT is not a specific technology; overall, it is a group of methodologies and implementations that help make all these "things" much smarter.

For example, the smartwatch you wear communicates with your cell phone to exchange data. An app inside your cell phone helps users extract information from a smart watch. The cell phone is also responsible for uploading the data to the cloud. With this, we can easily say that the "smartwatch" is a "thing" while the cellphone is an "edge device."

Note that we are not reinventing the wheel to develop IoT solutions. We are simply putting more elements on the wheel, which helps us explore IoT-specific use cases, like how you will change the tires to drive on snow. Now that we have an idea of IoT, let's walk through an actual example of how it is used daily.

Intelligent Vehicles

Nowadays, most cars we see on the road come with "connected tech." What this essentially means is that you can monitor your car and probably control it regarding cooling, engine immobilization, etc., from your cell phone. This is indeed one of the most useful implementations of IoT. But how does it work? Simply speaking, the car has something called as an ECU, which translates to electronic control unit. This ECU uses a protocol called Controlled Area Network (CAN) to communicate with various sensors and other key components. The ECU is also connected to the Internet using an e-sim. The ECU sends those data collected via the sensors. Thus, in this case, sensors send data to ECU, the ECU then sends the data to a communication unit which in turns sends the data to an IoT platform. What we see on our cell phones is essentially the data coming from an IoT platform. We can get more clarity through Figure 1-1.

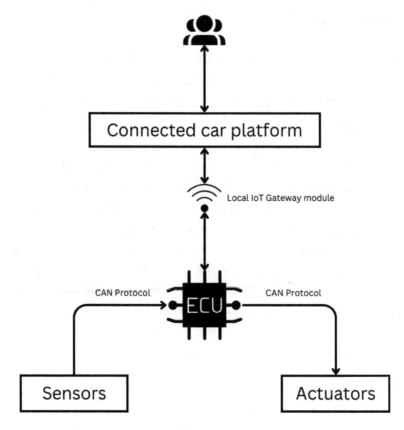

Figure 1-1. *IoT process in intelligent cars*

Typically speaking, an IoT system has a generic architecture, and we can approach the problem in a modular way. Ideally, IoT contains the following components:

- Sensors

- Actuators

- Controllers

- Gateways

- Platforms

- Applications

Every IoT system will consist of most of these sub-systems. In the world of IoT, another important concept to note is that "It's not just about hardware." Most of the folks I interacted with have this misconception that it's just about the hardware. Yes, that's an integral component, but it's not just the only component in IoT, and as a matter of fact, it's an amalgamation of both hardware and software systems. At a high level, an IoT system can be broadly represented or segregated into two major sub-systems:

1. Edge

2. Cloud

It's not necessary that all IoT systems will consist of the cloud component but they will definitely consist of the edge component. At a high level, we can refer to Figure 1-2 for better understanding.

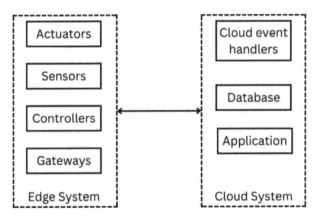

Figure 1-2. *High-level overview of an IoT system*

A Closer Look...

Let's walk through each component mentioned above and check out some examples of each one.

Sensors

Sensors are devices and systems that detect the present condition and changes in an environment, such as temperature, humidity, ambient light, pressure, etc. These devices can be analog or digital. Typically, an analog sensor will report changes in voltage and current levels, which reflect a physical change in the environment. However, a digital sensor will have an onboard controller to send the actual digital value of the perceived environmental parameter. Sensors are used all over the place in IoT as that's the only way we know a system's present status.

We're surrounded by sensors all around us. For example, smartwatches have a heartbeat sensor to measure our pulse rate. At our homes, we might have motion-activated washrooms or stairway lights. In an industrial system, we have tons of sensors doing a specific thing, such as temperature, pressure, contact point sensors, and more.

Actuators

Actuators are components that convert electrical signals to mechanical signals. They are the devices that interact with the actual physical system. Unlike sensors, which help a system understand environmental parameters, actuators help the system interact with the physical environment. Usually, actuators are responsible for some kind of physical motion. Some examples of actuators are electric motors and solenoids, and there can be different types of actuators like pneumatic, hydraulic, etc. Like sensors, these are also used widely in an IoT system.

Controllers

This is the most prominent component when it comes to the edge system in general. It is usually the brain of the edge system. It is responsible to collect data from sensors and perform some action in real time with the help of actuators. Usually speaking, it has the following functions.

1. Control the edge system

2. Interact with sensors

3. Execute real-time actions

4. Process the data at an edge level

5. Communicate further in the upstream

The controllers are responsible to send the data to the upstream to the gateway. An interesting thing to note is that sometimes controllers and gateways are a single device, which means that the controller has networking capabilities. This is very common in many hobby devices like ESP series, more commonly known as NodeMCU. In industrial systems, these are commonly referred to as a programmable logic controller (PLC) device which reads the data from sensors and performs some actions with the help of actuators. The PLC is then connected to another edge device, and data exchange happens through protocols like Modbus or CAN.

Gateways

Gateways, as the name suggest, are ideally responsible for handling all the communication of an edge system. These receive data from controllers and send it to the cloud upstream. These devices have networking components and usually support various protocols to both receive data and send data. Most of these devices are based on openWRT standard and can support protocols like Wi-Fi and LTE for upstream, and Ethernet and LoRa (long range) for receiving data from the controllers. Usually, these devices will have their own configuration portal which will enable these devices to be configured and also package the data accordingly. These devices also have the capability to send data back to the controller and support at least half-duplex communication.

Thus, from the above discussion, we can see the various components of an edge system at a high level. Let's briefly overview what the cloud system in IoT refers to.

The "Cloud" Part in IoT

The cloud computing era has been transforming the way how we build apps. With the advent of amazing cloud computing platforms available for use, this technology is virtually present in any solutions that involve software. When we develop any solution for the Internet of Things, it's in the best interest to make it cloud-friendly, and this means not only using graphs and charts. The cloud part of IoT refers to a whole set of functionalities and features needed to complete an IoT solution. It doesn't matter if you are a device manufacturer or some consumer; at the end of the day, having a cloud platform definitely adds a lot of flavor to the existing system. Some of the key components of the cloud in IoT are mentioned below.

1. Device management, including provisioning and over-the-air (OTA) updates

2. User management

3. Data management

We will discuss this in detail in a later chapter of this book. In addition to cloud computing, another key component is the end-user application, which may be available on web or mobile platforms. These are the applications that a user uses to interact with the system.

Types of IoT Systems

In the world of IoT, there is no proper terminology for what exactly can be termed an IoT system. Sometimes, a smart industrial automation system is often termed an IoT system. Technically speaking, in IoT, the letter I stands for Internet. However, in the greater schema, we can broadly classify IoT systems into two types:

1. Local connected ecosystem (Intranet based)

2. Globally connected ecosystem (Internet based)

However, in 99% of the use cases, it's usually a combination of both, which is referred to as a hybrid system.

High-level architecture

Now that we have a general idea about some of the basic components of an IoT system and what each component does, let's have a look at the basic high-level architecture diagram (Figure 1-3) of a typical IoT system.

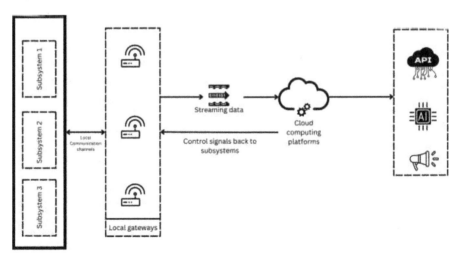

Figure 1-3. *A typical architecture of an IoT system*

You can broadly classify the above architecture into three stages.

1. Stage 1: Edge layer

   a. Subsystems

   b. Local gateways

2. Stage 2: Cloud layer

   a. Streaming data

   b. Cloud computing platforms

3. Stage 3: Application layer

   a. API

   b. Data intelligence

   c. Notifications

Stage 3 and Stage 2 can exist inside a cloud layer, but typically, it's the end-user application that is being referred.

The "Why" Factor

All this time, we have been focusing a lot on understanding what an IoT system consists of. We've also checked out one of the use cases using an intelligent vehicle scenario, but the question is why it is needed and whether it is just about IoT.

In the world of IoT, we deal with data and like any other technology, data is probably one of the most valuable assets in today's world. These data points are being generated from different sources and from different devices, and it is extremely important to analyze and understand this data. For example, if you have a smart watch that monitors your heart rate, the data captured from it helps you analyze your health and monitor your heart rate while resting or exercising. This will help you to plan your fitness routine accordingly. Similarly, in the case of a smart vehicle, vehicle parameters like fuel efficiency, engine temperature, and tire pressure help us to make decisions regarding the vehicle and whether servicing is needed or not. Again, in the world of smart industries, data generated from the factory floor helps to make intelligent decisions, optimize production, and do predictive maintenance on equipment.

What IoT does is simply provide the framework and the set of methodologies and protocols to achieve the same.

Conclusion

We have reached the end of this introductory chapter, and by this time, you should have a better sense of the basic idea of IoT. In the upcoming chapters, we will discuss each component, methodology, and protocol in detail.

CHAPTER 2

Getting Started with Edge Systems

Edge systems refer to all the hardware components of the Internet of Things ecosystem. From sensors to gateways, edge systems are responsible for data collection, forwarding it upstream, and taking some actions. However, edge systems can be equally complex, and it depends on the use case to determine their complexity.

This chapter will focus on the following, which will help us build the foundation of edge systems:

- Sensing

- Processing

- Communication

We will also build some small systems based on open sourced platforms to better understand the entire flow. These small systems will feature examples that illustrate the following:

- How sensors capture data

- How the data can be processed by a controller

- The various architectures and the networking concepts used

© Avirup Basu 2025
A. Basu, *Building IoT Systems*, Apress Pocket Guides,
https://doi.org/10.1007/979-8-8688-1212-5_2

- How to enable networking privileges using non-IP-based communication protocols

- How to connect a communication module to another device using a decentralized approach

Getting Grounded

Let's begin our journey on edge systems with one real-life example. Figure 2-1 shows a smartwatch sending some information to a cell phone using Bluetooth Low Energy (BLE), and the cell phone then syncs up with the cloud.

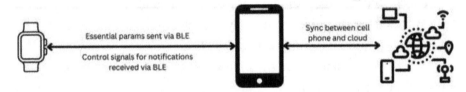

Figure 2-1. *Smart watch/cell phone communication with BLE*

The cell phone also sends control signals or notifications to the smartwatch. In this example, the combined smartwatch and cell phone will be called the edge system. There are a lot of strategies on how an edge system can be designed. As discussed in the previous chapter, an edge system will typically consist of the following:

- Sensors

- Actuators

- Controllers

- Communication unit

Industrial systems today consist of smart sensors, which are more commonly referred to as "IoT Sensors." These sensors consist of all the components needed to perform the computation on board and directly stream the values through a communication unit, which a gateway can pick up.

Defining Our System Specifications

To begin with, let's start with a system we want to build.

Problem statement: Record soil humidity values and switch on or off a pump based on those values. Please note that we aren't sending this data anywhere; thus, this system will be standalone.

Solution: Before coming to the exact solution, let's break the problem into different parts.

1. What parameters do we need to sense?

2. How will the sensor send the data, and where will it be sent?

3. What will be the communication medium between the sensor and controller?

4. What controller will we use?

5. How will the controller control the pump?

It seems like a complex problem, but it isn't. It's a straightforward problem with a simple solution. However, for every edge problem in IoT, it's essential to answer all these questions specific to the problem statement, which will help simplify the problem. Let's answer the above questions first and then refer to Figure 2-2 for an in-depth solution.

Parameter to sense: Humidity percentage

Sensors to be used: Any generic humidity sensor with digital output (DHT22)

Communication medium: Analog and digital channels

Controller to be used: Arduino platform or any other open sourced platform

Pump: Any low-voltage DC pump

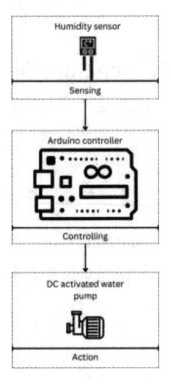

Figure 2-2. *System overview*

We still are unsure about a few factors, like whether there isn't any communication unit, whether it is even an IoT system, and how the humidity sensor will send values. To answer these questions, we need to break it down into three separate components (sensing, processing, and communication) and explain how each one interacts.

Sensing

We already had a brief overview of sensors in the previous chapter. Let's do a deep dive into understanding how sensors work and what to look for when considering an IoT sensor. Sensors in its simplest form convert raw environmental parameters to either a digital or an analog output but how does it work and what to look for in a sensor? When dealing with sensors, we look into the following:

1. How it detects the parameter we are trying to measure

2. What is the range of the sensor

3. What is the type of sensor

4. How to get data from the sensor

These four points help us select a sensor. Let's begin by understanding how sensors work.

Working of a Sensor

The working of a sensor may depend on the parameter it is trying to detect. We will take the example of a temperature sensor here. A temperature sensor essentially is a voltage-level sensor. It detects the temperature by reading the voltage or resistance level. It's usually directly proportional to the temperature, and thus, by measuring voltage, we can detect the temperature. These are typically called analog temperature sensor. Similarly, by detecting voltage and resistance levels, a lot of sensors can be developed. For example, an ambient light sensor uses a light-dependent resistor whose value again changes based on the light intensity. These help us in identifying the actual value by observing either voltage or current or resistance. Now, usually speaking, these sensors are very cost effective and usually require a lot less power, and thus, for the same reason, these sensors are used widely.

However, sometimes, the value can be directly obtained. Let's take another example of an ultrasound proximity sensor.

Ultrasound Proximity Sensors

As the name suggest, a proximity sensor measures the distance. There is no direct way to measure distances. You need an indirect way to measure the same. Ultrasound proximity sensor uses ultrasound waves to measure the distances using ultrasonic waves. Figure 2-3 shows how this works.

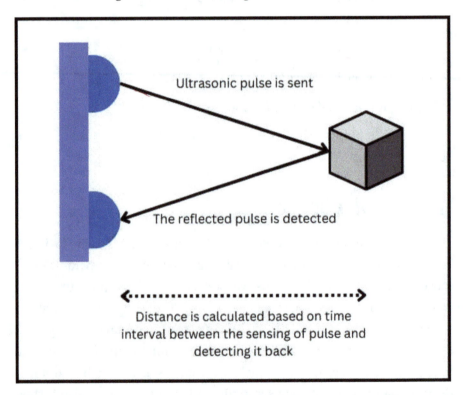

Figure 2-3. *Using a sensor to calculate the distance to an object indirectly*

In Figure 2-3, there is a sensor that is used extensively by students and hobbyists known as the HCSRO4 module, which does exactly what is mentioned above. A similar methodology is applied while detecting proximities using a laser or radio waves. These devices are more commonly known as LIDAR (laser detection and ranging) and RADAR (radio detection and ranging). LIDARs and RADARs are much more complex devices, but the base methodology is still the same as discussed above.

There are many more types of sensors that are available but one common entity between all the different types of sensors is simply the ability to detect a change in one parameter based on which we can get the value.

Additional Ways to Indirectly Detect

There are more ways to detect some parameters. For example, if we want to detect if a door is open or closed, what can be the possible solution? It can be done in many ways in fact. Let's have a look.

One of the most common ways to check if a door is open or closed is to use a specific sensor called "contact sensors." These sensors use a magnetic field to detect whether a door is open or closed. Based on the magnetic field strength and whether the circuit is closed or open, the inference can be drawn if the door is open or closed. Let's have a look at the diagram below to understand it.

Range of a Sensor

One important point to note while dealing with sensors is their range. A sensor built to detect temperature ranging from -30 to +70 degrees Celsius cannot be used in an environment to detect temperatures below -30 or above +70. We will have strange values in those cases, or the sensor might get out of order. Thus, it's crucial to know a sensor's range and understand if it fits according to the use case.

Getting Data Out from a Sensor

Using a sensor is one thing, but what do we do after we get the values and how do we get the values from a sensor? This chapter section will walk you through some of the high-level concepts of communication between a sensor and a controller. There are many different ways how this can be handled, and it all boils down to the fact of what the sensor supports. Let's have a look at the following scenarios:

1. Analog output

2. Digital output

3. Serial port communication

These three pointers are some of the most common ways to extract data from a sensor. However, there are more complex methodologies for advanced systems that will help us extract value from a sensor. These include protocols like Modbus, CAN, etc., but those are reserved for further chapters under industrial IoT.

In the case of analog output, we get a range of values and these depend on the analog to digital converter (ADC).

The range of the values received will be directly or indirectly proportional to the sensor value. For example, if we want to sense the intensity of light, we use a sensor called LDR, which stands for light-dependent resistor, and the value in resistance is what represents the intensity of light. These values are as we mentioned earlier depends on the ADC and its resolution. The next question that will come across our minds is what exactly is the resolution of an ADC?

Figure 2-4 provides an example of an Arduino just for simplicity.

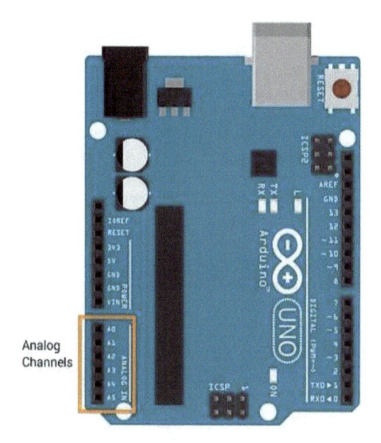

Figure 2-4. *Arduino analog channels*

Here, we see an Arduino UNO that has a total of six analog input channels. Thus, for the sensor, we can connect the output pin of the sensor to any of the analog channels. Now, for this Arduino, the ADC resolution is 10 bits which means that, it will give values ranging from 0 to 1023 (2^10) on these pins. When we are writing code on a controller to read these values, we read digital values, and even from analog pins, we read digital values which are the ADC-converted values. That is one way to read from a sensor.

Another way is when the sensor directly outputs a digital value. We can connect the sensor directly to any of the digital pins, which will give the value directly. In the above case of an ultrasonic sensor used to measure proximity, we read for pulses. Pulses are digital signals, and we can use any of the digital pins to read the value. Yes, there are some calculations involved to calculate the time, but at the core, it's all about reading for the pulses using digital signals.

That is how we use analog and digital signals to read from a sensor. Serial port communication is the third basic way to read from a sensor. The term serial port communication is a big term in itself, and we will discuss it in detail in the next chapter, which deals with protocols. However, it simply uses something called the universal asynchronous receiver-transmitter (UART) to transfer data packets to the controller from the sensor. Most of today's smart sensors rely on it. On top of UART, sensors can have their own software-based data formatting, which will wrap the actual data in a specific format and then send it across. For example, data formats like NMEA are used widely in GPS receivers. More formats like JSON can be used. It can also be a format specific to the manufacturer. Other than UART, there are additional ways through which a sensor can transmit through protocols like CAN or I2C. More on this will be discussed in the next chapter, which will discuss protocols.

Processing the Data

The first step is to get data from a sensor. The next step is to process the data and perform other critical decision-making tasks. These are done by a controller. What exactly is a controller? Well, in simple terms, it's the central brain of the edge part of an IoT system. There are easily more than a thousand controllers available in the market, but the choice of a controller depends on certain areas, and it's very specific to the use case. There might be a lot of situations where there can be more than one controller involved. While a deeper discussion on controllers is not the scope of this chapter, certain concepts must be discussed before moving further. In the world of IoT, there are two broad types of systems:

1. Industrial IoT systems

2. Commercial/consumer IoT systems

Ideally speaking, in the case of industrial systems, we don't have a high flexibility in the choice of hardware as the sensors and controllers are all industrial grade. Simply speaking, these industrial systems are primarily heavy-duty systems, and thus, a requirement exists to make the controllers resilient and sturdy. One of the primary requirements is the necessity of a real-time system. Now, getting to understand from a consumer/ commercial IoT systems, which also includes hobbyist IoT systems, many options are available. The most widely used controller, as showcased above in the sensor section, is an Arduino and its variations. For now, we will focus totally on these types of systems. To choose a controller, we need to understand the following specifications:

1. How many sensors need to send the data to the controller

2. What is the choice of networking

3. Power requirement

4. What is the computation power needed

If we can answer the pointers as mentioned earlier, then the process of selecting a controller to do a task also gets easier. In the most generic case, a controller will receive signals from sensors and extract meaningful information from those signals. A controller needs to be programmed, too, and thus, the choice of the programming language and its compatibility with the hardware also plays a vital role. However, most of the latest controllers built for these type of use cases support a multitude of programming languages, and thus, writing code to process the data is a lot easier. But, the question remains, why do we need to process the data or what is the actual reason behind it?

Let's take an example. In the above case of an ultrasound proximity sensor, we get the data in pulses. Some calculation needs to be done in a controller to compute the distance. Let's look at a sample code using the Arduino platform to see how it will be done if the sensor is connected to an Arduino board.

The pseudo-code is showcased in Listing 2-1.

Listing 2-1. Code overview

```
1. Initialize:
   - trigPin = 9
   - echoPin = 10
   - duration, distance

2. Setup:
   - Set pinMode of trigPin to OUTPUT
   - Set pinMode of echoPin to INPUT
   - Begin serial communication at 9600

3. Loop:
   - Set trigPin to LOW
   - Wait 2 microseconds
   - Set trigPin to HIGH
   - Wait 10 microseconds
   - Set trigPin to LOW

   - Measure duration of HIGH pulse on echoPin and store in
duration
   - Calculate distance = (duration * 0.0343) / 2
   - Print "Distance: " + distance to serial monitor
   - Wait 100 milliseconds
```

Let us walk through each step descriptively.

1. Initialise: Here, we initialize the pins to actual digital pins on the Arduino board.

2. Setup: Here we need to define whether the pins needs to be defined as input or output. In this case, the trigger pin will be set to output whereas the echo pin will be set to input. We also initialise the serial port communication where we can observe the values returned by the controller.

3. Loop: This is simply equivalent to an infinite loop. Here, the main logic is written. In this case, we send a pulse, wait for the echo pin to turn on, and then calculate the duration. Finally, we calculate the distance and print it out on the Serial monitor. The entire process is repeated once every 100 milliseconds.

This is one of the examples where the distance is computed in the controller. The same can be written in the Arduino framework (Listing 2-2).

Listing 2-2. Arduino code for distance calculation

```
const int trigPin = 9;
const int echoPin = 10;

float duration, distance;

void setup()
{
 pinMode(trigPin, OUTPUT);
 pinMode(echoPin, INPUT);
 Serial.begin(9600);
}
```

```
void loop()
{
 digitalWrite(trigPin, LOW);
 delayMicroseconds(2);
 digitalWrite(trigPin, HIGH);
 delayMicroseconds(10);
 digitalWrite(trigPin, LOW);

 duration = pulseIn(echoPin, HIGH);
 distance = (duration*.0343)/2;
 Serial.print("Distance: ");
 Serial.println(distance);
 delay(100);
}
```

This is a very simplistic example of a controller doing some calculation. In ideal cases, it will be responsible for a variety of tasks and will handle a variety of sensors. Here comes another important concept called as sensor data fusion which will be discussed later on.

Controllers come in various forms and sizes, some of which are shown in Figure 2-5.

Figure 2-5. *Some widely used controllers*

There can be scenarios where you need to use a single-board computer (SBC), something like a Rpi or other similar device, to work as a controller. These situations normally arise whenever there is some heavy processing involved like video or image processing. In these scenarios, the focus is given to computation power, memory, and networking capability of the devices.

Now that we have a generic understanding on controller, let's look at the networking and probably one of the key layers of IoT at an edge level.

Networking Layer

The key to building an IoT system is using networks at multiple levels. We have already seen some examples of how sensors capture data and how the data can be processed by a controller.

In this section, we will look at various architectures and discuss each in detail and some of the networking concept that is used. There are many strategies that are applied while designing IoT systems at an edge level. Some of these strategies involve direct communication to the Internet or through some gateway. Sometimes, several local networks are used to achieve connectivity. Whatever the scenario, a networking component will be involved. This brings to the fact that how do we take care of all the communication at an edge level. There are two major factors to consider:

1. The type of network needed for devices

2. The availability of IP-based connectivity devices

In the first section, we must understand how the devices can talk to each other. We will cover some of the related concepts. The next section will be a walkthrough of how the system as a whole or each device talks to the Internet in a decentralized manner.

How Devices Communicate with Each Other

Ideally, we can broadly divide a system into two major categories based on how it is designed and deployed. Figure 2-6 shows a centralized approach.

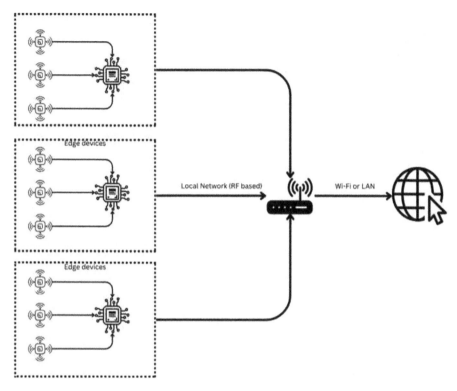

Figure 2-6. *A centralized approach to IoT*

Here, image sensors communicate with a gateway through any RF-based network like LoRa, ZigBee, Sigfox, BLE, or anything similar and the gateway then communicates to the Internet. This is a very common methodology and widely used in a variety of use cases like industrial IoT and home automation. If we do a deep dive of Figure 2-6, there are some open-ended questions:

- What protocols to use and when?

- How to identify edge devices?

- What network layer to use?

- What is a gateway and what to use?

To answer these, the first thing to note is what these local networks are and when to choose what.

Edge devices may contain either a sensor or a group of sensors sending data to the controller. It can be like temperature, humidity, and ambient light sensors sending data to a controller, let's say to an STM32 controller. These controllers come in a PCB package that contains IO pins that interact with the sensor. Ideally speaking, these controller packages can only process the data. They can't communicate. To communicate to a gateway, we can opt for any RF-based protocol, but to do the same, you do need to use a communication module. These modules are built specifically for transceiving data.

They receive the data and then use an RF protocol to send those data. These devices or modules are very specific to the protocols. For example, a chipset supporting LoRa may not support Wi-Fi, and a chipset supporting Wi-Fi may not support ZigBee. Thus, in every IoT project, it's essential to choose the protocol and the design at the very beginning. This way, the development will be faster and many costs will be saved. But how do we choose these devices, what criteria to look for, and what are the other options available? There are several factors to consider, and more than that, there are many modules available in the market. However, there are some specific protocols like LoRa where only one company manufactures the chipset and then a PCB is provided by other companies, which functions as an abstraction layer. Figure 2-7 illustrates it.

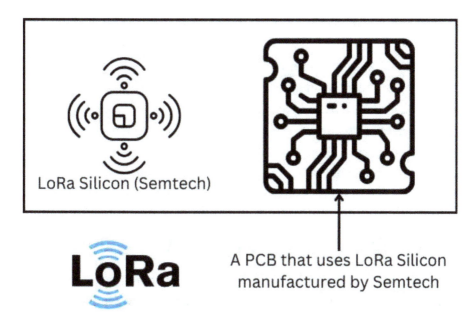

Figure 2-7. *Abstraction example of LoRa – concept of breakout board*

Essentially speaking, the actual LoRa module is manufactured by a single company called Semtech, while many other companies manufacture devices using LoRa silicon. These devices contain IO options for receiving data and connecting to antennas, power, etc. An image of a generic LoRa module is shown in Figure 2-8. It's manufactured by a company called Ai-Thinker.

Figure 2-8. *Breakout board*

This module internally uses Semtech's SX1278 IC. If you notice the image clearly, you will notice that there are options to connect IO pins to a controller like an Arduino or Raspberry Pi. At the same time, we also have an option to connect an external antenna. This is one example of a communication module that can be hooked up to another device thus enabling networking privileges. However, one important point to note here is that these are non-IP-based communication protocols. Hence, there needs to be a receiver that will act as a gateway in between to send the messages to the Internet, as illustrated in Figure 2-8.

Using a Decentralized Approach

Now, let's look at a concept using a decentralized approach. Here, each device can communicate with the Internet directly. Figure 2-9 illustrates this.

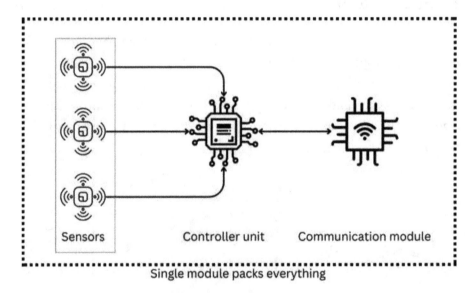

Single module packs everything

Figure 2-9. *Decentralized approach to IoT*

As you can see, it's just a single device or a combination of more than one device, but the most important point to note is that each controller and sensors combined communicates to the Internet using its own on-board communication module using either of the following ways:

1. Direct connectivity using e-sim or physical sim

2. Using Wi-Fi

Technically speaking, in case of Wi-Fi, the router works as a gateway and the device communicates with the router. However, in cellular-based communication, the device as a whole communicates to the Internet directly. This method is used in cases where the number of devices is less and the place where the devices are deployed has good connectivity. This is not suitable for cases with low connectivity or where we are dealing with a large number of devices as that would incur more costs. However, in the former case, since the number of devices is less, the cost factor is low as we don't have to buy a dedicated IoT gateway.

Some key pointers that we can conclude based on the above discussion are as follows:

1. If the number of devices is low, then using the gateway method is not economical, as IoT gateways are costly. In these cases, the single unit can directly communicate to the cloud.

2. If the number of devices is large (industrial IoT and home automation), then a centralized approach is better suited as individual devices (with RF protocol support) as it's more economical and the range can be extended using concepts like Mesh networks. A gateway will essentially provide the connectivity.

3. The choice of a local network is dependent on a lot of factors like range and the number of devices it will connect to. If the range is extremely widespread, LoRa provides a better approach. In other cases, if it's confined within a small space like a house, ZigBee offers a better solution.

4. Individual device power consumption is another key element to consider, as that will decide what to use and what to avoid. For example, cellular communication consumes more power than LoRa-based communication.

Conclusion

This chapter focused on the following edge features:

- Sensors

- Controllers

- Communication

A key factor is choosing the right networking approach, and building the solution depends on accessibility and cost. We did skip actuators for now, but you should have a foundational grasp of how each of these components works and what to consider while designing an edge system.

## CHAPTER 3

Machine to Machine (M2M) Communication

Machine-to-machine (M2M) communication is one of the most challenging parts of implementing IoT systems. The previous chapter briefly discussed how the system communicates with the cloud. This chapter's prime focal point is how two or more devices talk to each other, the methodologies involved, and how one can design such a system. We will also walk you through some of the protocols involved in M2M communication. If you recall the architecture of IoT systems, the part we will focus on is at the edge level. An ideal IoT use case would involve a lot of sensors and controllers all talking to each other via a local network. Here, let's dive deep into these networks and how devices can talk to each other, what protocols are available, what the strategies are, what to use when, and so on. A bunch of concepts will be clarified regarding M2M communication by the end of this chapter.

© Avirup Basu 2025
A. Basu, *Building IoT Systems*, Apress Pocket Guides,
https://doi.org/10.1007/979-8-8688-1212-5_3

Communication

Many factors exist to enable communication between devices, which helps us determine what technology or protocols to use. At a high level, we will consider the following cases:

- Wireless non-IP-based technologies are widely used, including ZigBee, LoRa, BLE, etc., whereas IP-based technologies, which are used by almost everyone, are Wi-Fi.

- There are wired technologies, too, used mainly for communicating in a closed and constrained environment, such as sensors to controllers or within two or more controllers in the same system. These include protocols like CAN, I2C, etc.

- Finally, we have communication to the cloud, which is done either by Wi-Fi or through cellular communication like LTE, LTE-M, 5G, etc.

We will cover each area in detail and walk through some of the scenarios to get an understanding of what is supposed to be used where. Before we do, though, let's quickly review some key concepts.

Modulation and Demodulation

We all use wireless communication in our daily activities. Whenever we deal with any form of wireless communication, modulation and demodulation are some of the key concepts that make this transmission of signals possible. So, what exactly are modulation and demodulation?

Modulation is the process of varying a carrier signal (such as a radio wave) to encode information (data) and efficiently transfer the signal over a medium, either wired or wirelessly. Demodulation, similarly, is how we can extract the information (data) from the modulated signal. The following are the types of modulation most commonly used:

- Amplitude modulation

- Frequency modulation

- Phase modulation

A simple example of amplitude modulation is shown in Figure 3-1.

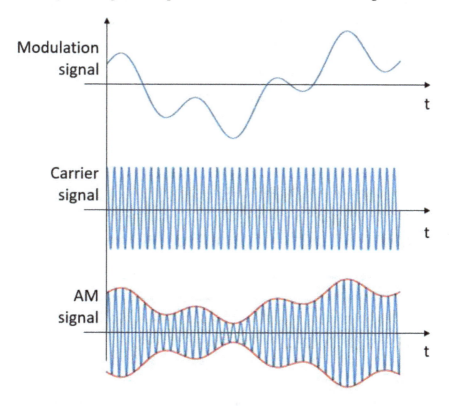

Figure 3-1. *Amplitude modulation*

As shown here, the carrier wave carries information about the information signal by varying its amplitude. Since the amplitude is changing, this is called amplitude modulation. Thus, the frequency gets modulated, and the phase gets modulated in case of frequency and phase modulation, respectively.

Simplex, Duplex Communication

Simplex is a one-way communication system in which data can flow only in a single direction. Radio and television broadcasts are examples of this. Duplex is a bidirectional communication system in which the data can flow from one node to another node and vice versa. However, this can be subdivided into subcategories:

a. Half duplex: It's a type of communication where the sender can receive signals but not at the same time. An example of this will be walkie-talkie systems.

b. Full duplex: In this, a sender can transmit and receive at the same time. The example of such system is mobile communication systems.

Selecting an M2M Communication System

What protocol to use and what system to opt for while designing an M2M communication system is very important. There can be situations where we need to focus on bandwidth, or in some cases, the focus can be on network coverage. Sometimes, the network needs to be developed for constrained systems or in some cases the traffic will be high, and reliability may be a major consideration. There are many cases in which the proper communication system needs to be selected. The following are some important considerations to consider while designing such systems:

- Power requirements

- Bandwidth requirements

- Frequency requirements

Power requirement is a major consideration in the world of communication systems. For example, suppose you are developing a system in which sensors must be placed in remote locations where constant power is unavailable. In that case, a battery may be the only option.

Now, some wireless technologies provide very good bandwidth but are not very economical regarding power management while some others may not be very good in terms of bandwidth but extremely efficient in power management. Thus, it's important to consider when selecting the technology. Bandwidth is also another key factor to consider. Depending on the network traffic, a decision needs to be made on the same. Bandwidth refers to the amount of data that is sent or received over a particular period of time. Some network may be good in bandwidth and not much power efficient and vice versa.

Finally, one of the most important factors is the frequency requirement. A network may operate under a certain frequency which may not be legal or licensed in the geographical region or it may interfere with other devices. Thus, making sure that the frequency selection follows all the local wireless rules and regulations and doesn't interfere with the existing devices is crucial. Thus, from the above discussion, it should be clear how the three pointers play a key role in selecting a wireless communication technology.

Low-Power Wide-Area Network (LPWAN)

LPWAN as the name suggests is a class of low-powered networks developed specifically to facilitate building of wireless network for the purpose of IoT. This type of networking concept came into practice with the launch of Sigfox and LoRa which was eventually followed by NB-IoT. As of today, most of the IoT systems are based on LPWAN. Some of the key characteristics of LPWAN are mentioned below.

Long Range

This is the most significant feature of LPWAN and the reason why it is used so widely. Unlike traditional technologies like Wi-Fi, LPWANs can cover a distance ranging from a few meters to tens of kilometers. This makes them a perfect choice to be deployed in rural and remote areas. However, in case of an urban environment, the typical coverage area ranges from 1 to 5 km depending on a lot of factors including density of buildings and other concrete obstacles.

Low Power Consumption

These networks are designed for constrained systems, and thus, as discussed earlier, power consumption is taken very seriously here. In these networks, the power consumption is usually low. This allows it to be used specifically with battery-operated devices. Ideally, devices that use LPWANs can function from several months to years on a single battery charge cycle. Thus, for this reason, the usability of this technology is high in constrained devices. However, the battery consumption is extremely dependent on how the device is being used or programmed. For example, the battery life will be much more in case the device periodically transmits signals rather than always transmitting.

Low Data Rate

A single network cannot always be this good. There has to be some trade-off; in the case of LPWAN, that trade-off is its low data rates compared to other technologies. This trade-off is acceptable, depending on the use case. The low data rate is beneficial in cases where signal is transferred infrequently over a certain period of time. In these scenarios, the data packet is also on the lower side.

Scalability

Another key advantage of LPWAN is that it can support a large number of devices within a singular network infrastructure. This is beneficial for IoT deployments involving thousands, perhaps millions, of connected devices. These networks are designed to handle a high density of IoT devices, making them robust for large-scale IoT applications.

Examples of LPWAN Technologies

The following are some of the most commonly used LPWAN technologies:

- LoRa (Long Range): A protocol stack developed by Semtech that is particularly popular when it comes to devices spread across a large area. This network operates on the ISM band.

- Sigfox: It's a global network operator which uses ultra-narrowband technology to provide long-range connectivity with a minimalistic power consumption. These are also based on the ISM band. This network is known for its simplicity, and thus, it's one of the most popular choices for IoT projects.

- NB-IoT (Narrowband IoT): NB-IoT is developed
  by 3GPP (3rd Generation Partnership Project) and
  is a standard based on LPWAN. It operates within
  a licensed spectrum and is designed to work with
  existing cellular networks.

There are more examples of LPWAN, such as RPMA (random phase multiple access) and weightless.

Note   ISM stands for Industrial Scientific Medical. This frequency band is reserved specifically for these purposes and doesn't require licensing. Examples of wireless technology using the ISM bands are LoRa, BLE, Wi-Fi, RFID, etc.

Why LPWAN for M2M?

LPWAN has many characteristics that are well-suited for M2M communication, as discussed earlier. However, in some cases, LPWAN may not be useful, especially where the data rate needs to be on the higher side. LPWAN is a set of technologies that were built with IoT in mind as, in the world of IoT, we deal with constrained devices, and because we usually don't have to deal with a high data rate, LPWAN works out great. However, LPWAN is not suited for cases where we need to deal with real-time systems. LPWAN prioritizes on uplink (device to network) communication and may have limited downlink capabilities. Real-time systems on the other hand require a full-duplex communication in most cases, and downlink is always a priority. In these cases, we prioritize low latency, and for the same, a trade-off is perfectly fine in terms of power and other advantages provided by LPWAN. LPWAN is mostly used in the following cases:

- Environmental monitoring: Monitoring of environmental parameters such as air quality, soil monitoring, etc.

- Smart metering: Used for monitoring utility meters and sending data in regular intervals

- Asset tracking: Tracking location of assets over long distances

In all of the above cases, a point to note is that we really don't care on the signal latency and the frequency of transmission is also low. Thus, these are the perfect examples where LPWAN can actively be used. However, for real-time systems like that of controlling an assembly line (industrial automation) or that of a vehicle's ECU (electronic control unit), the delay in transmission can't be considered. In these cases, we do need minimal latency and high reliability, and thus, LPWAN can't be used in these cases. Wi-Fi, BLE, and ZigBee/Z-Wave are examples of such.

Protocols for Real-Time Systems

What are real-time systems? To understand some of the protocols used in real-time systems, which are an essential part of M2M communication, let's first understand what a real-time system is.

In the context of IoT and M2M communication, these are those systems that require data to be transmitted and processed within a specific time period strictly. These systems provide timely responses. Time is of the key essence here. Here are some characteristics of such systems:

- Timeliness: These systems must respond to inputs or events within a specific time period. This is extremely crucial for applications where delays can't be considered.

- Determinism: The system's behavior should be predictable to specific inputs. The output should be expected and defined and should happen within a defined time-frame.

- Reliability: High reliability is often required for these systems as failures aren't an option here, especially in mission-critical systems like industrial automation and healthcare.

- Concurrency: These types of systems handle multiple events or data stream at the same time. Thus, the network should be capable of handling it and have effective ways of concurrency management.

In the case of these systems, let's have a look at some of the protocols. These protocols can be classified into wired and wireless. Under wireless, we have the following:

- Wi-Fi: This requires no introduction, but it is used in systems like smart appliances specific to home automation and industrial monitoring. However, it is not very efficient regarding power management and has a limited range.

- Bluetooth Low Energy (BLE): It's a short-range communication protocol designed for low power consumption. It is used mainly in wearable devices and smart home devices. It's mainly suited best for short-range communication. However, the data rates are also on the lower side.

- Zigbee: Zigbee is a low-power, low-data-rate wireless mesh protocol primarily used for home automation, smart lighting, and, to some extent, industrial automation. However, data rates are lower, and the range is shorter than Wi-Fi. Its usability in a mesh configuration is often advantageous in scenarios similar to home automation.

Some of the wired communication protocols are widely used in the industry.

- Modbus is a serial communication protocol built for the industry based on the client-server architecture. It is widely used with PLCs. However, Modbus can't truly guarantee real-time performance.

- CAN: It stands for Controlled Area Network. It was developed by Bosch, and its specific purpose is to be used in automobiles and vehicles. However, CAN is also used in industrial automation. CAN allows two or more controllers to talk to each other without a hosted controller. It is very reliable and has real-time capabilities.

There are more wired protocols that can be used for example, I2C which are used to read sensor data. Figure 3-2 lists some of the widely used protocols in the world of IoT.

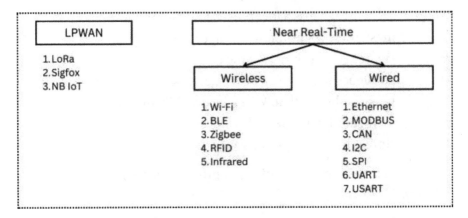

Figure 3-2. *Protocol list for IoT*

What Protocols or Technologies Do You Use?

We have a fair understanding of some of the protocols used in IoT. However, with such a large number of protocols and technologies, it's easy to get confused about what to use when. Let's try to simplify this by understanding how devices communicate at each layer. Based on specific parameters, it will be simpler to determine the technology. Let's have a look at the following scenarios.

Scenario 1: Building a Weather Monitoring Station

Multiple strategies can be used, but for the sake of example, we will stick to one. We want to build a wireless weather monitoring station powered by a battery. In this case, we just want to deploy a single unit.

We can immediately say that we need some form of cellular communication here as a mesh or other wireless network may not be economically viable. Thus, the following should be applied:

1. Cellular communication may be used.

2. Message needs to be sent periodically.

3. LPWAN like NB-IoT can be used if network connectivity is available.

Scenario 2: Monitoring Industrial Equipment

When it comes to monitoring industrial equipment, we often need near-real-time data. For this reason, we always prefer a system with a constant power source. Another important point is that most industrial sensors may not be able to transmit data directly. They may need a gateway. Ideally, the process illustrated in Figure 3-3 is normally followed.

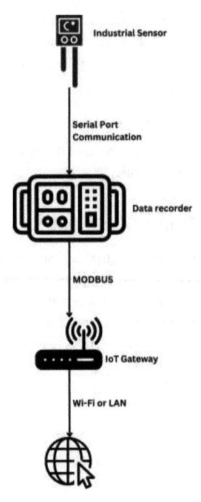

Figure 3-3. *High-level data flow from sensor to cloud*

Here, we see that we use a combination of protocols:

- Serial port communication

- Modbus

- Wi-Fi or Ethernet

The advantage of such a system is that multiple sensors can be connected to the data recorder using a real-time protocol, and the data can be transferred to a gateway using Modbus to an IoT gateway. The structure in Figure 3-3 is used in most industrial monitoring systems.

Scenario 3: Smart Agriculture Monitoring

When it comes to monitoring agricultural land, it is spread across a large area, but at the same time, many sensors are present. In those cases, adopting the first strategy, where individual systems communicate directly to the Internet, may be inefficient. Thus, a mesh network or a network consisting of LPWAN is a good choice here. In these cases, most of the new modern-age sensors use LoRa. LoRa sensors communicate to a LoRa gateway, and then, the gateway in a very similar way communicates to the cloud.

Based on the discussion of the above three scenarios, we have a fair idea of what wireless technology to use and when. That said, selecting an M2M communication system generally needs to satisfy some generic requirements irrespective of the technology we opt for.

- Message delivery for sleeping devices: In the case of IoT, not all devices are always active. Some devices may wake up periodically and then send data to the cloud and then again go to sleep. This is usually done to preserve power. When communicating with devices that have an inbuilt sleep functionality, sending data isn't a problem. However, if you want to communicate back to the device, that creates a challenge. This needs to be looked into while selecting the network for M2M communication.

- Message acknowledgement techniques: In many cases across the M2M communication ecosystem, messages may get dropped, leading to data loss. Thus, there needs to be an appropriate methodology for confirming message delivery. In case of a failure, the message can be resent.

- Algorithm for message routing: Another key aspect of M2M communication especially with respect to mesh networking is traffic routing. What it means is if there are multiple devices spread across a network, how a message is routed to a gateway is something that needs to be looked into.

- Notification in case of communication failure: In these cases of communication failure, we must consider how the admin will be notified of a failed node or a failed message. An efficient algorithm will prevent the loss of data and handle duplicate records.

- Managing devices and OTA: We will discuss OTA in detail later in this book, but at a high level, a process should exist for managing devices and their firmware remotely through the network or cloud.

- Scalability: It is a key factor especially in terms of industrial or commercial deployment. The network should be capable enough to scale up or scale down based on devices and network traffic.

- Security: The network should be foolproof in terms of network security and intelligent enough to handle external attacks. Additionally, the aspect of data encryption must also be considered while designing the solution.

In most cases as seen above, it's a combination of multiple technologies and protocols that constitutes an IoT system. You might use LoRa or ZigBee or CAN and then use cellular or Wi-Fi to connect to cloud. In almost every case, it's a combination of multiple networks.

If you look at it from a different angle, we are also surrounded by a similar gateway-based architecture in everyday life. For example, we are connected to Wi-Fi routers, which are connected to the optical fiber network. Similarly, when we use cellular connections, our cell phones are connected to the nearest BTS – base transceiver station – and that actually provides the network connectivity. Thus, in everyday life, we use devices with different protocols to connect to a global network.

In the above discussion, we have seen the different wireless technologies and protocols that are being used. The following list summarizes them:

- Non-IP based (wireless):

    a. LoRa

    b. ZigBee

    c. Sigfox

    d. BLE

    e. RFID

- Non-IP based (wired)

    a. UART

    b. USART

    c. I2C

    d. CAN

    e. Modbus over the serial port

- IP-based (wired)

  a. Modbus over TCP/IP

  b. Ethernet

- IP-based (wireless)

  a. Wi-Fi

  b. NB-IoT

Thus, in a typical M2M design, we might end up using multiple technologies involved at each level.

Conclusion

In this chapter, we had an overview and general understanding of an M2M system. This will help you to design better IoT systems. Please note that the list of technologies available keeps on changing and while designing an IoT system, it's best to opt for the best available technology and not the latest available technology. Sometimes, the best may not be the latest. Thus, depending on several factors like power, frequency, coverage, etc., as discussed above, it's best to do thorough research on the best technology to opt for. In one of the upcoming chapters, when we deal with projects, we will see how this is played out in real life.

CHAPTER 4

IoT Data Communication Protocols

In the last chapter, we saw some of the technologies used and some protocols for IoT communication. Here, we address a different section of IoT communication protocols: the data section and protocols implemented on TCP/IP or WebSockets. These are essentially different ways of transferring data and are widely used in IoT and software development in general. Figure 4-1 showcases our interest areas.

- Device to cloud (D2C): This refers to all kinds of communication from a device to the cloud for sending any kind of data. Telemetry data sent from a device to the cloud is an example.

- Cloud to device (C2D): This refers to the cloud sending data back to a device. This can be of any form like sending responses to the device or sending control signals.

© Avirup Basu 2025
A. Basu, *Building IoT Systems*, Apress Pocket Guides,
https://doi.org/10.1007/979-8-8688-1212-5_4

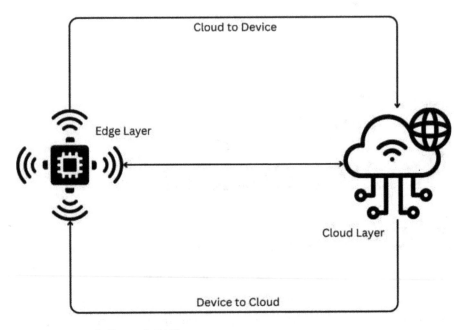

Figure 4-1. *C2D and C2D process*

In this chapter, we will cover some of the most widely used protocols in the industry.

HTTP REST API(s)

Representational State Transfer (REST) is an extremely flexible protocol based on a design and software architecture style used to access data on the web. It relays to IoT with devices sending data to the cloud (Figure 4-2). In short, the devices send data to a remotely hosted web service.

> R: Representational
>
> S: State
>
> T: Transfer

Together, it makes REST. This refers to a set of design and software architecture style that is widely used in creating services based on the web. It is very useful to access data on the web and is an extremely flexible protocol.

But how does it relay to IoT? Well, in the case of IoT, we deal with devices sending data to the cloud. What is a cloud? It is a set of machines located remotely and hosting some services. Thus, essentially, the devices send data to a remotely hosted web service.

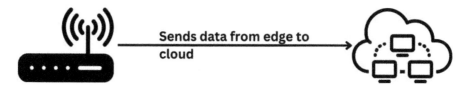

Figure 4-2. *REST API high-level flow*

Depending on the use case, there are other ways too; however, let's keep the focus on REST for now. This protocol is much more robust than Simple Object Access Protocol (SOAP) as it uses less bandwidth and is extremely flexible. Here are some of the key concepts of REST API:

- Resources: These represent entities or objects in your system. Each resource in here is uniquely identified by an URL.

- HTTP methods:

    a.   REST API uses some standard HTTP methods to perform operations on resources:

        i.   GET: Retrieve data

        ii.   POST: Create a new resource or data point

        iii.   PUT: Update an existing resource or data point

        iv.   DELETE: Remove a resource

        v.   PATCH: Partially update a resource

- Statelessness: Each request made to the server should contain all information. By default, the server doesn't maintain any information about the client. At an application level, this can be made to retain some information.

- Uniform interface: A consistent and standardized interface is used to interact with all the resources. These includes the use of standard HTTP methods and status codes.

REST API has its own set of advantages:

- Scalability: The REST API structure is based on the client server architecture. This means that it's stateless, which enables the server to handle a large number of client requests.

- Flexibility: Clients and servers can be developed independently. This means that different sets of technologies can be used to do the same. (We will discuss on this later.)

- Simplicity: The use of standard HTTP methods and status codes like 200,500,400, etc., helps in the development of applications using these protocols.

Using REST in IoT

In the world of IoT, REST APIs are used actively in the following scenarios:

- Communication between edge devices and IoT platforms: This is applicable when different devices send data to IoT platforms, which are essentially web services, and some IoT platforms support the use of REST API.

- Configuration of a device - remote management: Some of the devices need to communicate with the platform to obtain the device configuration (more on this will be discussed in the IoT Platform chapter). Usually, these operations are done using REST APIs.

In a properly implemented IoT solution, devices send data to cloud not using REST API but all other operations of the device communicating with cloud services are done using REST APIs. Additionally, at the cloud layer, almost everything happens over REST API calls as it provides a lot of flexibility. Another important use case where REST API is actively used is during an OTA update on the devices.

Essentially speaking, REST APIs are used actively in device-to-cloud (D2C) communication. The reason why C2D or cloud to device is not possible is that the devices normally do not have a fixed address; they are just clients. Thus, hosting a publicly available web server on these devices is not a very optimized way of achieving C2D. This is where we get introduced to the pub-sub model; specifically, we are interested in MQTT.

Message Queue Telemetry Transport (MQTT)

MQTT is a pub-sub model actively used in the Internet of Things. It's a lightweight protocol designed for constrained systems. MQTT is the go-to protocol for all data-related communication protocols, including D2C and C2D messaging. Figure 4-3 illustrates a simplified diagram, which consists of the following components:

- MQTT broker

- MQTT clients (MQTT publisher and MQTT subscriber)

- MQTT topics

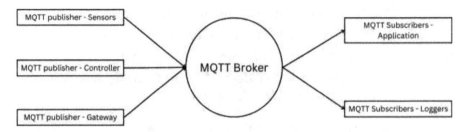

Figure 4-3. *MQTT architecture – high-level diagram*

Figure 4-3 is one of the most simplified diagrams on MQTT. It consists of the following components at a high level:

- MQTT broker

- MQTT clients

    a. MQTT publisher

    b. MQTT subscriber

- MQTT topics

As mentioned earlier, MQTT works on a pub-sub architecture, and like all pub-sub architecture, the overall concept of what it is and how to use it remains the same. In these cases, there is one centralized broker and then there are clients. A client can again be a publisher, a subscriber or both. MQTT sends messages in topics and these help to segregate out the messages we are interested in. Let us dig a bit deeper and see what each of these components refers to.

Broker

MQTT broker is essentially a centrally hosted server which is the main component. All MQTT clients are connected to the broker. It receives messages from publishers and sends it to subscribers. It is responsible for performing the following key responsibilities:

1. Message routing:

    a. Receive and route messages: The broker receives messages published by clients and routes them to all clients that have subscribed to the corresponding topic.

    b. Topic matching: The broker matches messages to subscriptions using topics, which can include wildcard characters for flexible subscription patterns.

2. Session management: Handling client connections, disconnections, and maintaining session states.

3. Quality of Service (QoS): Ensuring messages are delivered according to the specified QoS levels.

4. Security: Implementing authentication, authorization, and encryption mechanisms.

Topics

A topic is a UTF-8 string that represents a message route. Topics are hierarchical, with levels separated by forward slashes (/), for example, home/living room/temperature.

- Topic structure: Topics can have multiple levels, allowing for organized and structured message routing. For example, building/floor/room/sensor.

- Wildcards: MQTT supports two types of wildcards for subscribing to multiple topics:

    - Single level (+): Subscribes to one level of the hierarchy. For example, home/+/temperature matches home/livingroom/temperature and home/kitchen/temperature.

- Multilevel (#): Subscribes to all subsequent levels.
  For example, home/# matches home/livingroom/
  temperature and home/kitchen/humidity.

Note   Wildcards are very important and are widely used to manage, route and log messages. This will be clearer when we implement the actual project later in this chapter.

MQTT Clients

MQTT clients are applications that run in either a device or software which connects to a MQTT broker. Clients can act as publishers, subscribers, or both.

- Publisher: A client that sends messages to the broker on specific topics.

- Subscriber: A client that receives messages from the broker on topics it has subscribed to.

Clients are responsible for establishing a connection to the broker, maintaining the connection, and handling messages appropriately. A lot of libraries exist in different programming languages for connecting to brokers.

Quality of Service (QoS)

MQTT messages define a total of three QoS to ensure the reliability of delivering the messages.

1. QoS 0 (at most once): The message is delivered at most once, with no acknowledgement. This is the fastest and least reliable level.

2. QoS 1 (at least once): The message is delivered at least once, with the receiver required to acknowledge receipt. This ensures the message is received, but it may be delivered multiple times.

3. QoS 2 (exactly once): The message is delivered exactly once, using a four-step handshake process to ensure no duplication. This is the slowest and most reliable level.

The QoS is essential, especially when it comes to telemetry data.

Retained Messages

A retained message is a message that the broker stores and delivers to any new subscriber to that topic. It ensures that new subscribers receive the most recent message immediately upon subscribing.

Last Will and Testament (LWT)

LWT allows clients to specify a message the broker will send if the client disconnects unexpectedly. This feature is helpful for detecting failures and taking corrective actions.

Persistent Sessions

Persistent sessions allow clients to maintain their state between connections. The broker stores the client's subscriptions and any undelivered messages, ensuring they are delivered when the client reconnects.

Security

MQTT includes various security mechanisms to protect communication:

- TLS/SSL: Transport Layer Security (TLS) or Secure Sockets Layer (SSL) encrypts the data transmitted between the client and broker, ensuring privacy and data integrity.

- Authentication: Clients can verify their identity by logging in with the broker using username/password, certificates, or other methods.

- Authorization: The broker controls which clients can publish or subscribe to specific topics, ensuring that only authorized clients can access certain data.

There are more aspects to MQTT security but it's usually broker-specific. However, at a high level, just consider that authorization can be done against a database.

A Closer Look at Brokers

Let's have a look at some of the most widely used MQTT brokers.

Eclipse Mosquitto

- Open source: A lightweight and widely used open source MQTT broker.

- Features: Supports all MQTT versions, WebSockets, TLS/SSL, and authentication mechanisms.

- Use cases: Suitable for small to medium-scale applications and development environments.

HiveMQ

- Commercial and open source: Offers both open source and enterprise versions.

- Features: High performance, clustering, enterprise security, and extensive management tools.

- Use cases: Ideal for large-scale and mission-critical IoT deployments.

EMQX

- Commercial and open source: A scalable and highly available MQTT broker with clustering support.

- Features: Supports MQTT, MQTT-SN, CoAP, LwM2M, WebSockets, and more.

- Use cases: Suitable for large-scale IoT applications with high throughput and reliability requirements.

Project Use Case: (Simulated Smart Agriculture)

Now that we understand what REST APIs and MQTT do, let's walk through one small project and see how each component works. This will involve simulated devices to get a generic understanding. Please note that the point of this project is to understand how both REST APIs and MQTT are used in a device to achieve desired results.

The following are a few things to consider:

1. We will use Python as a base language for the following:

    a. Web server to respond to request

b. Data logger to log the incoming telemetry data

c. Simulated device

2. We will use a globally hosted MQTT broker (HiveMQ) to connect to MQTT.

So, let's get started with the project.

We have the following requirements:

1. The cloud will configure the simulated device. The configuration will include the MQTT details and the parameters it needs to send as telemetry information.

2. The simulated device will perform the following actions:

a. Get MQTT-related data from the API

b. Get the parameters it needs to send to the MQTT

c. Send telemetry data to the MQTT broker

3. The API will perform the following actions:

a. Send MQTT and other configurable data points to the device

4. The logger will perform the following actions:

a. Receive telemetry data from MQTT

b. Update a JSON file with the data

Figure 4-4 represents the system.

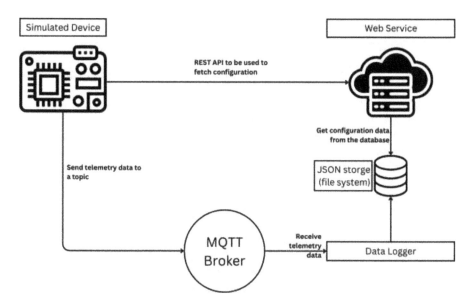

Figure 4-4. *System diagram*

Now, let's have a look at the JSON data that will be saved in a JSON file.

Saving the Data

In a real use case, we will have an actual database. The following JSON represents the device-related information that will be shared by the web service through REST API response.

```
{
    "device_id":"123AP09",
    "configuration":{
        "mqtt_config":{
            "host":"",
            "port":"",
            "publish_topic":"",
            "subscribe_topic":""
```

```
      },
      "parameter_config":["temperature","humidity"]
   }
}
```

In the above JSON, we have the following keys.

1. Device id

2. Configuration

   a. Mqtt configuration

   b. Parameter configuration (these are the parameters we want)

Now that we have the JSON, save the above JSON in a file named "device_config.json". Next, we will write a simple Python Flask code to serve the requests.

Create a new file named "app.py" and keep it in the same folder. Here, we are not going into the full details of the code but the code is simple enough to understand. It's a simple Python code that uses flask to serve requests.

```
from flask import Flask, jsonify, abort
import json

app = Flask(__name__)

# Read the configuration data from the JSON file
with open('device_config.json') as f:
    config_data = json.load(f)

@app.route("/config/<string:device_id>", methods=['GET'])
def get_config(device_id):
    if device_id == config_data["device_id"]:
        return jsonify(config_data)
```

```
else:
    abort(404, description="Device not found")
if __name__ == "__main__":
    app.run(debug=True)
```

We have a method named get_config which checks if the incoming device_id is same as the one in the configuration file, and based on this, the API sends back the JSON as a response.

On executing the above codebase, we open any API testing toolkit and trigger a GET request which is a REST API call. This is triggered by the device to the web server. As a response, we will get the above JSON mentioned before. Now, the question is, if the role of the API is just to send back the config JSON, why do we even need it?

That is a valid question. To answer it, think of a situation where you have deployed a total of 100 devices. All of these devices are connected to a MQTT broker and send some data. The broker details are configured within the devices. Now for some reason, the broker is changed, or the configuration has changed. In that case, all 100 devices will be affected. Thus, in these cases, we keep a centralized authentication server and we use that server to pass on the configuration file-related information.

Figure 4-5 shows the response received as triggered from the POSTMAN.

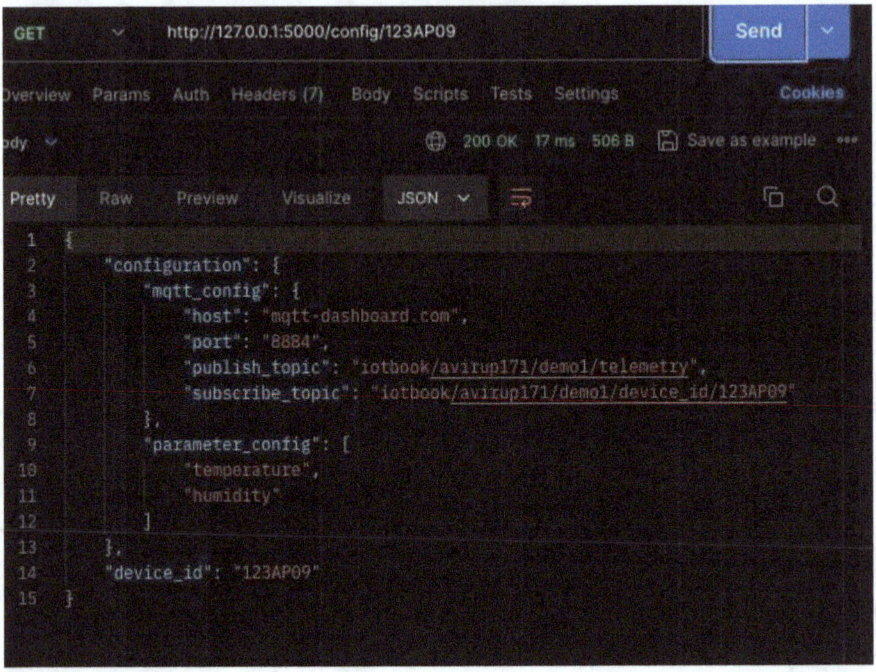

Figure 4-5. *POSTMAN response*

Now, how do we use this information and its configuration? Let us assume the following:

1. The simulated device can send the following parameters as telemetry data:

   a. Temperature

   b. Humidity

   c. Pressure

2. The simulated device contains the configuration fetch URL, which is http://127.0.0.1:5000/config/{dvcie_id}.

3. The device_id of the simulated device is "123AP09".

Now, the following are the actions to be performed by the simulated device:

1. To receive configuration parameters

2. To send telemetry data to the MQTT broker to the publish topic

3. To receive control information, if any, through the subscribed topic

Let's write a Python code for the above simulated device:

```python
import requests
import paho.mqtt.client as mqtt
import random
import time
import json

# URL to get the config file
config_url = "http://127.0.0.1:5000/config/123AP09"

# Get the configuration from the URL
response = requests.get(config_url)
if response.status_code == 200:
    config = response.json()
else:
    print("Failed to retrieve configuration.")
    exit(1)

# Extract MQTT configuration
mqtt_config = config["configuration"]["mqtt_config"]
parameter_config = config["configuration"]["parameter_config"]

# MQTT broker details
mqtt_host = mqtt_config["host"]
```

```
mqtt_port = int(mqtt_config["port"]) if mqtt_config["port"]
else 1883  # Default port 1883
publish_topic = mqtt_config["publish_topic"]

# Callback when the client receives a CONNACK response from the
server def on_connect(client, userdata, flags, rc):
    client.subscribe(mqtt_config["subscribe_topic"])
    print("Connected with result code " + str(rc))

# Callback when a message has been published
def on_publish(client, userdata, mid):
    print("Message Published with mid: " + str(mid))

# Callback when a message is received
def on_message(client, userdata, msg):
    print(f"Received message '{msg.payload.decode()}' on topic
    '{msg.topic}' with QoS {msg.qos}")

# Initialize MQTT client
client = mqtt.Client()
client.on_connect = on_connect
client.on_publish = on_publish
client.on_message = on_message

print(mqtt_config["subscribe_topic"])

# Connect to the MQTT broker
print(mqtt_host)
client.connect(mqtt_host, mqtt_port, 60)

# Start the loop
client.loop_start()

try:
```

```
while True:
    # Create a dictionary with random values for the
    parameters data = {param: random.randint(10, 100) for
    param in parameter_config}

    # Convert the dictionary to a JSON string
    payload = json.dumps(data)

    # Publish the message
    client.publish(publish_topic, payload)

    # Wait for a second before sending the next message
    time.sleep(1)

except KeyboardInterrupt:
    print("Script terminated by user.")

finally:
    # Stop the loop and disconnect
    print("Loop stopped")
    client.loop_stop()
    client.disconnect()
```

In the above code, we use the Paho MQTT library to connect to the MQTT broker. We also use the requests module to trigger the HTTP GET request to the server we showcased earlier. We are not going into the full details of the code, but overall, we used methods as described in the Paho MQTT to handle connection-related events.

Additionally, in the above code block, we are using an infinite while loop to publish the messages to the topic. Interesting to note is the fact that all the configuration-related details are fetched using the API call. This includes the MQTT details and publish and subscribe topics.

The above code can be executed by typing

```
python simulated_device.py
```

This will publish the messages in the topic mentioned in the configuration file. You can use any MQTT client to visualize the results. Figure 4-6 shows the incoming stream of messages.

Figure 4-6. *mqttX used as an MQTT client*

Conclusion

Thus, from the above discussion, some of the concepts related to data protocols are a bit clear, especially with respect to HTTP, REST, and MQTT. More than the protocols in general, it's important to understand when to use what and when not to use what. There are other protocols too like AMQP, but at a high level, we usually deal with these. In terms of actual implementation, most IoT platforms release their own software packages which implement these at a low level. However, the upcoming chapter will be focused on the cloud side of IoT and we will eventually see how platforms work.

CHAPTER 5

Cloud Computing

Up till now, we have focused on the edge layers and the communication layers. As we move forward in the world of IoT, we now venture into the world of cloud computing. Well, the fact is, without cloud computing, IoT won't be the Internet of Things but the Intranet of Things. The fact that devices can be monitored and controlled remotely is all possible due to cloud computing. This chapter will be focused on cloud computing and some key concept areas. At the end, we will have a sneak peek into building of an IoT data pipeline taking Azure as an example.

Introduction to Cloud Computing

Cloud computing refers to the usage of computational services like servers and databases over the Internet. It's essentially using software which are hosted remotely somewhere else. This approach allows developers and businesses to access the technology and resources on demand remotely without the necessity to use physical computation resources.

Let's take a simple example to address this. For example, there are two options when hosting a website:

1. You buy a dedicated PC and run the website on the PC. The PC needs to be on 24×7 and must have a static IP address.

2. You simply provision a VM in one cloud service and deploy your website there.

Which one will you choose?

For the first, you need to do a considerable amount of investment to maintain the above. In the second one, you just pay for the amount of resources you consume. We would definitely go for the second one. Similarly, in the case of IoT, devices need to send data to somewhere upstream. In these cases, we provision some group of cloud services and the device will send the data to those cloud services through some methods.

Cloud computing is the base of IoT. However, one may argue that why is it needed? Can't we do the same as mentioned in the above point (1)? That may be true, depending on the use case. However, ideally, we would go for a cloud approach.

The following are some of the benefits of cloud computing:

- Cost savings

- Scalability

- Flexibility

- Improved collaboration

Based on the above, almost every application has something to do with cloud computing.

The following are just a few of the cloud computing services:

- Infrastructure as a service

- Platform as a service

- Software as a service

- Function as a service

Let's take a look at each of these now.

Infrastructure as a Service (IaaS)

This type of cloud computing provides virtualized computing resources over the Internet. It is probably the most basic form of cloud computing, and essentially, it's the base of any cloud computing platform. With this, businesses can rent IT infrastructure like servers, storage, and network providers from a cloud provider on different payment models like pay as you go model. The following are some of the IaaS providers:

- Azure Virtual Machine

- DigitalOcean Droplets

- Google Compute Engine

- Amazon Web Service Elastic Compute Cloud

Platform as a Service (PaaS)

This type of cloud computing provides a platform allowing the users to develop, run, and manage applications without dealing with the underlying infrastructure. This saves a lot of time for developers to setup the systems for their software(s) to run. Essentially, with PaaS, developers can focus on the actual application than worrying about the deployment. The following are some of the examples:

- Azure App Services

- Google App Engine

- Netlify

- Heroku

Software as a Service (SaaS)

This type of cloud computing provides virtualized computing resources over the Internet. It is probably the most basic form of cloud computing and essentially the base of any cloud computing platform. With SaaS, you can work on the application side rather than developing it. We use SaaS almost every day in one form or another. Some examples of SaaS are Google G Suite, Microsoft Office 365, etc.

Using Cloud Computing in IoT?

Cloud computing forms the backbone of IoT, and the IoT pipeline, which is key to developing any solution, consists of the following (see Figure 5-1). Therefore, each layer should be targeted accordingly.

- Edge layer (data generation)

- Processing layer (messaging hub)

- Storage layer (data sink)

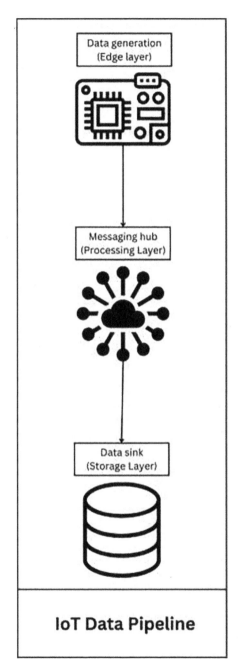

Figure 5-1. *IoT data pipeline*

This is what we call an "IoT Data Pipeline." It will always be relevant when developing solutions for IoT.

As discussed above, the major three components of an IoT data pipeline consist of a data generation unit, which is the edge layer, and the processing and storage layers, both of which are part of cloud computing. We have already discussed in previous chapters how edge devices send data. Here, let's focus on the remaining two layers, which are the processing and storage layers.

Processing Layer

The processing layer is where all the data processing happens. It consists of endpoints where the edge devices can connect to and send data, as well as internal functions where we do the actual processing. In the previous chapter, we talked about protocols like MQTT and REST. In the case of IoT, this processing layer will internally consist of many subcomponents, depending on the requirement. The main part of the processing layer is business logic, which is very specific to use cases. It may involve simple data write operations or it may also involve operations involving multiple operations happening in parallel.

Let's have a look at some components or key areas that are handled by the processing layer:

- Data processing

- Data analytics

- Business logic orchestration

- Data visualization and reporting

- Integration with external services

Data Processing

In IoT, data processing refers to the set of operations that transform raw data from IoT devices into meaningful insights, actions, and outcomes. It plays a crucial role in any IoT system. Sensors generate vast streams of data which needs to be processed before saving, and these are normally a computation intensive process. These systems are based on cloud, and ideally speaking, the main advantage of using it is that the device dependency for processing is reduced. Let's have a detailed outlook of how it works. To begin with, let's have a look at the types of data processing:

- Edge processing: This we have already covered in the last chapter where we do the processing of data at the edge level based on certain situations and then send the data to the cloud. This is mainly done to reduce the latency and obtain real-time processing. Edge processing is common and is used widely in some form or the other.

- Real-time processing: Real-time processing is essential for applications that require an immediate response such as industrial monitoring, healthcare systems, smart cities, and more. The target is to reduce the latency to a great extent. The data will be processed as soon as it's available downstream from the edge device. There are a lot of technologies that can be applied in real-time processing. Some of the examples are mentioned below:

  a. Apache Kafka

  b. AWS Lambda

  c. Azure functions

  d. RabbitMQ

Real-time processing is used widely and at the later part of this chapter, we will see how this can be achieved using Azure.

- Batch processing: When the data volume is large and there isn't any need for real-time processing, we would opt for batch processing. However, there are a lot of scenarios, for example, data analytics, where batch processing is the only option available. For batch processing too, there are a lot of open source technologies that are available for use.

- Hybrid processing: In 90% of IoT systems, we deal with hybrid processing which is usually the combination of more than one type. Some part of the system will need real-time processing while others like predictive maintenance will be dealt with batch processing. Thus, whenever we design an IoT system, we primarily think through what is the type of data and what is the type of use case, and based on that, we decide what will be real-time or what will be hybrid.

Data Analytics

In the world of IoT, we often deal with huge amounts of data and raw data means nothing unless there is some form of meaning to it. Data analytics is widely used to understand the raw meaning of data. This is where we do a deeper analysis on the incoming stream of data and understand how the system is performing. This usually involves several statistical methods, data mining, or machine learning techniques.

- Descriptive analytics: This is just like a summary of the data. An example of such will be average temperature or humidity over a certain period of time.

- Predictive analytics: It simply uses historical data to predict future outcomes or trends.

- Prescriptive analytics: It again relies on the past data and recommends possible actions.

In IoT, data analytics plays a key role, as without it, it's difficult to understand a system and how it will perform.

Business Logic Orchestration

The implementation of business logic is another key important step. The processed data is sent to this layer where business logic check happens. Every single use case needs a business logic that drives automated workflows and actions. Based on these, there can be two scenarios.

1. Event-driven architecture: Most of the IoT systems follow an even-driven architecture, where specific conditions or events trigger actions. For example, sending an alert or changing the thermostat settings of HVAC when the temperature changes beyond a certain threshold.

2. Automated workflows: Based on some predefined rules, the system can automate tasks like scheduling maintenance, adjusting parameters, or sending notifications.

Business logic layer is one of the most important elements in the world of IoT.

Please note that business logic is defined across various layers, namely edge and cloud. Real-time implementation goes into edge while non-real-time implementation happens at cloud level.

Data Output and Visualization

Once data is processed and analyzed, it is often presented to users or integrated into other systems for further action. Either the data can be shown in real-time, or it can be shown in the form of historical charts and graphs. Dashboards form a key role in the cloud computing part of IoT. However, these are more application specific and rely on the use case. For example, in the case of an industrial system, we do need real-time monitoring. However, for others we might just rely on historical data.

Integration with External Services

Data visualization is one part. However, we need capabilities in cloud computing where data needs to be sent to external services like an ERP, CRM, or any other third-party services. These usually mean the platform we chose for the system or whatever we design must have capabilities to send data. Usually, these are done through API calls. For example, we need to send data to salesforce if an alert gets triggered. In this case, salesforce will expose an API which the cloud computing platform will consume. This integration is usually done at the business logic layer.

Building an IoT Data Pipeline in Azure

We have a generic idea of cloud computing and its various components specific to IoT. In this section, we will understand the flow of data from edge to database through a cloud computing platform, Microsoft Azure. Let's get started with the basics, as in the components that are needed, but before going there, what is Azure?

Azure is a cloud computing platform by Microsoft, which provides a lot of out-of-the-box offerings. With respect to IoT, we are interested in some of the services that will help us to send and save data upstream. Azure is used in a variety of systems starting from application development to data engineering and from IoT to advanced AI and machine learning. Let's now take a closer look at the following components that are relevant to IoT ecospace:

- IoT Hub

- IoT Edge

- Azure Functions

- Any PaaS DB offerings like PostgreSQL

- Azure Blob Storage

- Azure Stream Analytics

Understanding the Components

Before deep diving into any solution, we must understand what we're dealing with in terms of individual components. At a very high level, the entire solution can be divided into the following parts:

- Edge device

- Messaging broker

- Data processing

- Data sink

Data processing can be done both at edge and at cloud, and it's usually split between the two. Based on the above classification, we can architect any IoT solution based on any cloud providers. In this case, we will stick to Azure and see how each component fits in the abovementioned classifications. The whole point is to understand the data flow from edge to cloud.

1. Azure IoT Hub: It is a messaging broker specifically built for not only acting as a centralized messaging hub but also enabling device management and reliable communication at an extremely large scale.

2. Azure IoT edge: It is a device-focused runtime that enables us to build, deploy, run, and monitor containerized Linux workloads. As the name suggests, it runs on supported edge devices and everything is manageable from the Azure cloud.

The above two IoT Hub and IoT Edge runtime are IoT-specific offerings of Azure. There are more offerings too like Azure IoT Central but that is not within the scope of this chapter.

Let's have a look at the other components that will be covered as a part of this chapter.

Azure functions: These are managed microservices that does a specific job. These have different triggers and can have different sinks too. Many languages, like C#, Python, Java, JavaScript, and more, are supported within function apps.

Azure stream analytics is a fully managed stream processing engine designed to handle and process large volumes of streaming data. Different scenarios can use ASA. It is also available at the edge, where it is known as Azure Stream Analytics for Edge.

These two components are a part of the business layer to process the data. Now, let's have a look at the data sink or storage options. There are multiple ways through which this can be achieved. Let's have a look at some.

Azure blob storage: It is a solution to store any kind of object. Most importantly data which is mostly unstructured. It's optimized to handle massive amounts of data.

Azure Cosmos DB: It's a fully managed NoSQL and RDMS for modern highly scalable application development. It's highly scalable and offers "single digit" milliseconds in response time.

Other managed solutions exist, too, like SQL and PostgreSQL, and those operate in a similar way to how native solutions behave.

Now that we know the components and where they belong, let's recap through Figure 5-2.

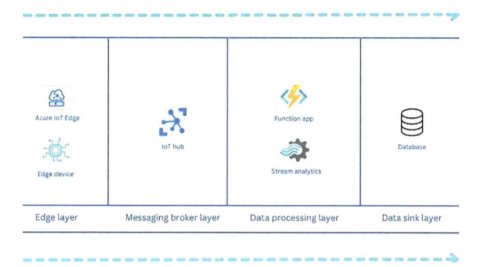

Figure 5-2. *Azure data pipeline*

Conclusion

In this chapter, we had a generic understanding of how cloud computing works and its role in the world of IoT. We have also seen how Azure can be used to build an IoT data pipeline. These are the few concepts that are used almost regularly in any IoT-based application.

GPSR Compliance
The European Union's (EU) General Product Safety Regulation (GPSR) is a set
of rules that requires consumer products to be safe and our obligations to
ensure this.

If you have any concerns about our products, you can contact us on

ProductSafety@springernature.com

In case Publisher is established outside the EU, the EU authorized
representative is:

Springer Nature Customer Service Center GmbH
Europaplatz 3
69115 Heidelberg, Germany